Contents

Extreme reptiles

Think you know everything about reptiles? Think again! Most reptiles have scaly skin, and can't make their own body heat. But the differences between reptiles are what make them **extreme**.

This gecko's weird body shape helps him to hide.

Some reptiles have bizarre bodies. Some behave in weird ways. These features help them to find **mates** or food – or avoid getting eaten themselves!

Never hug a boa!

Could you swallow a goat in one gulp? This is no problem for a boa. These huge snakes coil around their **prey** and squeeze it until it can't breathe. Like all snakes, they swallow their meal whole.

One large meal will fill a boa up for six months.

DID YOU KNOW?
Anacondas are boas that live in water. They are the largest snakes in the world.

7

Sneaky snakes

Small snakes make tasty snacks for **predators**. This coral snake does not need to hide from predators. Its bright colours warn that it has a deadly bite.

Killer crocs

Saltwater crocodiles are the largest reptiles in the world. They are powerful **predators**. Crocodiles have the strongest bite of any animal. Being caught in a croc's jaws would be a bit like being trapped under a large car.

DID YOU KNOW?

Saltwater crocodiles can grow up to seven metres long. That's about one-and-a-half times the length of a car!

Experts at escaping

There are more than 4,500 types of lizards. Some have **extreme** tricks to avoid getting eaten. A gecko doesn't panic if a **predator** grabs its tail. It runs away and leaves its tail behind. Then it grows a new one!

new tail

DID YOU KNOW?
A basilisk lizard's feet move so fast, it can run across water!

13

Horned lizards **distract** enemies with a disgusting trick. They squirt blood from their eyes! They do this by bursting **blood vessels** around their eyelids. The jet of blood can travel more than one metre.

When an Australian frilled lizard is in danger, it opens its neck frill like an umbrella. This makes it seem bigger.

Cross-eyed chameleons

Chameleons are famous for changing colour. One of the reasons they do this is to **camouflage**, or hide, themselves.

long, sticky tongue shoots out to grab **prey**

Chameleons have **extreme** eyes. They can point in different directions! They can look out for danger and dinner at the same time.

17

Turtle power

When the alligator snapping turtle gets hungry, it sticks its weird tongue out. Fish think that the tongue is a wriggly worm. But it's a trap. When they come to have a nibble, the turtle's jaws go snap!

tongue

DID YOU KNOW?
Leatherback turtles can hold their breath for more than one hour.

19

Komodo dragons

These fearsome **predators** are the heaviest lizards on Earth. They have jagged teeth like a shark and a **venomous** bite. Komodo dragons knock over big animals and then rip their **prey** to pieces.

venomous
spit

Tough tortoises

Nothing can bite through the shell of a giant tortoise. This helps them to live for more than 100 years. One pet tortoise even lived to celebrate his 255th birthday!

DID YOU KNOW?

The giant tortoise has a flat nose that helps it to drink through its nostrils. This helps it to suck up water from very shallow pools.

Awful alligators

Alligators look heavy and clumsy. But these reptiles can spin their bodies like ice skaters. The famous death roll helps alligators to tear **prey** into chunks. They bite their prey and then spin around really fast. They can rip off an arm or a leg in seconds.

powerful
tail

webbed
foot

Terrible tuataras

Tuataras have three eyes! The third eye can only be seen when they are babies. No one knows what it is for. It may help young tuataras to avoid their parents. Adult tuataras will eat their own babies!

third eye hidden under skin

tail drops off if attacked

DID YOU KNOW?
Tuataras have been around since the time of the dinosaurs.

Record-breakers

Which reptile do you think is the most **extreme**? Why? Have a look at some of these record-breaking reptiles to help you decide.

What? Chameleon

Why? Longest tongue

Wow! Some chameleons have tongues one-and-a-half times as long as their bodies!

What? Leatherback turtle

Why? World's heaviest reptile

Wow! The biggest turtle ever found weighed over 900 kilograms, more than some cars!

What? Saltwater crocodile

Why? Largest reptile

Wow! Males can grow up to 7 metres long, but most are hunted by humans before they get this big.

What? Small-scaled snake

Why? Most **venomous** snake

Wow! These Australian snakes have enough venom to kill 100 adults!

What? Spiny-tailed iguana

Why? Fastest reptile on land

Wow! This reptile from Costa Rica can run at 35 kilometres an hour. That's about the same as a top 100-metre sprinter.

What? Dwarf gecko

Why? Smallest reptile

Wow! Dwarf geckos measure about 16 millimetres from nose to tip of the tail. That's not even as wide as a £1 coin!

Glossary

blood vessel tube in an animal's body that blood moves through

camouflage colours or markings that help an animal to blend in with the things around it

distract draw somebody's attention away from something

extreme unusual, amazing, or different from normal

mates two animals that can have baby animals together

predator animal that hunts other animals for food

prey animal that is hunted by another animal for food

saltwater living in salty water

venomous able to produce venom. Venomous animals have a poisonous bite or sting.

Find out more

Books

Animal Disguises (Discover Science), Belinda Weber (Kingfisher, 2011)

Deadly Reptiles (Wild Predators), Andrew Solway (Raintree, 2005)

Killer Snakes (Animal Attack), Alex Woolf (Franklin Watts, 2011)

Snakes and Lizards (Really Weird Animals), Clare Hibbert (Arcturus Publishing, 2011)

Websites

Watch clips of the world's deadliest reptiles and other animals:
www.bbc.co.uk/cbbc/shows/deadly-60

Get face to face with komodo dragons:
www.bbc.co.uk/nature/life/Komodo_dragon

Play wild games and read animal books online:
www.zsl.org/kids/

Index

BETTWS 21·5·13